Facing Toward the East

Poems of Redemption

Books Previously Published by Carroll S. Taylor

Chinaberry Summer, New Plains Press 2013

Chinaberry Summer: On the Other Side, New Plains Press 2017

Feannag the Crow, Catch the Spirit of Appalachia, Inc. 2020

Ella's Quilt, Catch the Spirit of Appalachia, Inc. 2023

Plays Previously Written and Performed

Beneath the Sky and Waters, a One-Act Play co-written by Carroll S. Taylor and Raven Chiong, performed in April 2022

An Appointment with the Year Monger, written by Carroll S. Taylor, performed in February 2024

Facing Toward the East

Poems of Redemption

Carroll S. Taylor

Redhawk Publications
The Catawba Valley Community College Press
2550 US Hwy 70 SE
Hickory NC 28602

ISBN: 978-1-959346-57-9

Library of Congress Control Number: 2024940008

Printed in the United States of America

Layout by Melanie Johnson Zimmermann

redhawkpublications.com

Dedicated to my husband Hugh

Table of Contents

Epigraph

Facing toward the East:
For the dead, hope for the resurrection.
For the living, hope for redemption and renewal.
For all creatures, hope for a new beginning,
rising each day with the morning sun.

Miss Rose

Her car buzzed down our dirt road,
kicking up a cloud of red dust.
Daddy shook his head.
All that woman does is stay in the road.

I'd have stayed in the road, too,
if I was married to Mister Jobe.
He drank whiskey like sweet tea.
The day before she stood with him
in front of the justice of the peace,
she announced to her friends
she was going to change his ways.

She must've been changing his ways
in town, for all we ever saw
was her either coming or going.
On days when rain fell sideways
unchecked from angry clouds,
the wheels of her faded Ford
slung mud every which away
as they struggled to stay in the ruts.

Maybe she was changing him at night
when no curious neighbors could see
her work her magic on a man who
loved his liquor more than life.
A man who had no intention
of being remade different.

He was her third husband.
Everybody wondered:
Was she marrying men for love
or looking to fix the world
one old drunk at a time?

Facing Toward the East

Who will come to visit us?
Who will bring us flowers?
Who will stoop to brush
away brown leaves
scattered across our names
or to straighten vases
toppled by autumn winds?

Surely not the young ones.
They are far too busy
fidgeting with electronic gizmos,
posting pointless selfies.
They see no value in the past
when they can enjoy their now.

Their parents will be consumed
with shuttling children to games,
or with work and school
and household worries.
Their days are spent on the living.
They may find no reason
to visit in remembrance.

The children we were
wandered together
in our country cemetery,
each grave with a story to tell
of a life well lived or perhaps
a life that squandered its gift.

An innate unease lay silent,
embedded in our DNA,
the certainty of our own mortality,
knowing an eternal mystery

lies ahead for each of us.

We noticed faded flowers
and carved headstones
standing like punctuation marks
at the ends of sentences.

Two sisters, giggling together,
a bit of childish irreverence,
paused to read words written
for people we did not know.
We asked our mother:

Who was she?
And who was he?

Mama told us the story
of each one of them
after she ended her visit
at her father's grave.

Who will tell *our* stories?
What will we leave behind
for future storytellers?

We who are alive
should not fear
facing toward the East,
gazing at the morning sky
as rays of light radiate
above the cloud-dotted horizon,
revealing to us the promise
of a new day of life,
a renewal of faith.

Ancient people knew
and understood,
as should we:
The East is the direction
of eternal hope and grace.
Every morning is a rebirth.

Who among the living
will face the rising sun
with fierce determination?

Dawn breaks before us
with its urgent message
too precious to ignore:
Tempus fugit.
In our own time, in our own way,
we will all find ourselves
facing toward the East.
May our exclamation points declare:
Do not waste! Do not waste!

Ashes

When Miss Lurie died,
not a soul came to her funeral
because she never had one.
She didn't go to church anymore.
Nobody there knew she was gone.

Her family didn't call the preacher.
Seems they didn't see the point
in spending good money on a fancy
dress or taking time to write
her obituary for the newspaper.

Her son had her body cremated.
The family received her ashes,
but they still owed the funeral home
seventy-five dollars,

money they didn't have.
They managed to put down
a small payment every month or so,
but there she rested—unnoticed

on a shelf in the back of a closet
along with her collection of old, faded hats,
mothball-infused furs with staring, dead eyes,
and scarves dotted with spots of gravy and lipstick.

One woman's existence condensed down
to a shiny coffee can filled with a lifetime.
Her ashes, now on credit, sitting forgotten,
waiting for redemption.

Miss Dorothy

She had an air of being sad and out of place,
like an old tinsel Christmas wreath
left hanging on a porch in March.

Dressed in layers on a bright Georgia afternoon
in summer when the heat hung
    like muscadine vines strung across
    low branches of loblolly pines.
Even when the snakes were coiled tight
    under bushes to stay out of the sun.

A flowery headscarf tied under her chin,
she was always mumbling to herself
like she was part of the world
but the world wasn't part of her.

Her husband had died some years back.
Left her all alone in a rambling old house.
Somebody said she was a teacher.
Other folks said she was a witch.
Nobody really knew.

Strangeness doesn't make people
    good or bad.
Sometimes it just makes them lonely.

I tried talking to her one fall afternoon.
She wore a faraway look in her eyes.
I figured she was only a lost soul
    wandering along a red dirt road.

Persimmons piled in her basket,
    smooth golden yellow orbs.

Sassafras leaves shaped like mittens
turned red and orange.
And a blush-colored pomegranate
  on a bed of white oak acorns.

I didn't see her around for days.
The sheriff checked on her,
  but nobody was home.
Somebody said she had a son
  in North Carolina.
Somebody else said maybe she just
  up and disappeared.
Mostly, nobody seemed to care.

Edna

Born the middle child of eleven.
Out of school by sixteen
    to work in the cotton mill
    and marry her sweetheart.

Birthed five children during the Depression.
Widowed at forty-six with a farm to run.
But there were always books
on dusty shelves
and in closet nooks
behind flowery curtains.

Mystery and romance novels
taken to bed like lovers
on thundery nights
    when rain pelted the windows
    and lightning flashed.

Her slice of heaven
was a crumpled cardboard box
    filled with dog-eared books
    from a second-hand shop.

Lunch was a potful
    of white butter beans
    with a thick slice of fatback
    simmered on her wood stove
and buttermilk cornbread
    baked in a cast-iron skillet
    till the edges turned
    golden brown.

Her granddaughter learned to scramble eggs
on that same stove
by the time she was five,
standing in a wooden chair,
swirling the whites and yolks
in a cast iron skillet
until the eggs turned into breakfast.

The farm proved a refuge for
animals that had lost their way:
the unwanted,
the neglected,
the abused.

A pony that didn't like children.
A goose that hated men and pinched
the flesh halfway up their legs
before her victims could escape.
A young bull that stood on his hind legs
to nibble leaves off trees.
A duck who was in love with a rooster.
A rooster who spent time with a pig
and died two days after his friend
passed away in his pigsty.
A green parakeet that whistled at ladies.
A menagerie of cats.
Always a faithful dog or two
asleep in front of the fireplace.

Time well spent making memories:
Pulling taffy made with molasses.
Playing rainy day games.
Swinging on the front porch.
Mending a hoot owl's broken wing.
Telling stories passed down for generations.

Edna would go without food if she had to,
    but not one of her critters would go hungry.
Not one of her grandchildren
    would go without a book.
No one left her kitchen
    without a cup of coffee.

Loving animals
gave her purpose.
Loving her grandchildren
brought her delight.
Loving books
let her travel the world,
even on stormy nights.

Andrew

Wispy cotton feels light as a cloud
floating high in a blue Georgia sky,
but clouds are heavy, especially dark ones,
and sometimes they bring storms.

He'd found a refuge
from another storm—
The Great Depression.
Got himself a farm
with Roosevelt's New Deal.

Walking down pathways
of snowy white cotton,
surveying all the work that lay ahead,
he knew the back-breaking labor
would be impossible for one man.

Once, he promised his children a quarter
if they would pick a full sack of cotton.
He laughed a bit inside, knowing
his quarters lay safe, nestled in his pocket.

The three of them spent hours
dragging the rough picking sack
over dusty red dirt, trying in vain
to fill its six feet of canvas.

Wincing and sweating, fingers throbbing,
they handled sharp, piercing bolls
and dodged swarms of biting insects
under glaring sunlight.
They understood their father's ruse.

Everybody had to help with the cash crop
to make money for their food and clothes.
Farm animals and humans alike had to eat.
Though their contributions would be slight,
they would have a hand in their own destiny.

His vegetable gardens were bountiful.
President Roosevelt visited The Valley Project,
and Andrew became its *Farmer of the Year*.
All he could do was work the land,
pray for more soft rains to fall,
and hope fewer boll weevils
would find their way to his cotton.

But something far worse than weevils
laid a curse on that field in '45.
DDT dust drifted over row after row.
It had to be good—the government said so.

Andrew carried a duck cloth bagful
of it around his neck, the strap
crossed over his shoulder,
and sowed poisonous powder
on tender plants with his bare hands.
He sent it out in a hand-pump sprayer,
not as a blessing, but as a lethal malediction
leaving fine layers of death everywhere.

As he lay dying at fifty-three,
he smiled at his wife one last time.
He left his years of hard work,
the farm, fields, and dust behind
for his family to take up the struggle.

Now he walks in peace
in Elysian Fields.

A Message in a Garden

Papa raised dahlias.
Not just any dahlias.
His flowers were the size
    of bright red dinner plates
    and amber-orange saucers
floating atop tall, leafy plants.
    Or so the little girl remembers.

Dazzling garnet blooms by the back door
    and more in the yard.
Pink and lavender ones by the front porch
    rising near the daylilies
    and the English dogwood.
Lemon yellow blooms at the edge
    of the vegetable garden,
    smiling at their sister sunflowers
    and welcoming the friendly twirls
    of sky-blue morning glories
    on thin vines climbing upward
    as if to get a better look,

    as if their day-morn trumpets
    hoped to reach the top
    to revel among the vibrant colors
    and touch the flowers' faces
    before the glories had to close
    and fall asleep.

He fell ill in May,
and by late August he was gone.
    It was as if his dahlias
    understood and bowed
    their heads in grief.

The little girl did not understand
where her grandfather had gone.
She did not know the new word
spoken by the minister:
      Resurrection.

She helped her grandmother
      work in his garden.
      This dahlia is dead.
Her grandmother pulled it from the ground
      and tossed it with fury
      into the wild brush
      at the edge of the woods.

They plucked away any plants
      bearing sorrowful flowers.
Snatched them from the soil
      with bitter grief for the one
      they had given
      back to the earth.

Three days passed,
      and when they returned
      to their work,
something bright and beautiful
      caught their eyes:

A radiant, glorious dahlia
      the color of a summer sun,
      blooming with unbridled joy,
      facing the sky
      on its wilted stem lying uprooted,
      cast away in thick weeds.

Oh, look! We thought it was dead,
but now it's blooming.

And in that moment,
the little girl
understood the word
resurrection.

Benevolence

My father watches me
from his nursing home bed.
A puzzled look shades his blue eyes.
I recognize that expression.

I see it every time I visit.
He's thinking about my brother.
He wants to ask,
Do you think he had to work today?

My brother died years ago
by his own hand.
My father knows that—
or he *did* know that
before his latest stroke.

Weeks of fog and confusion
have shrouded his once-sharp mind.
His bitter memory has drowned itself
in a deep trough of sorrow and loss.
He has found peace at last.

Do you think he had to work today?
He asks again, expecting a reply.
How can I tell him the truth?
I cannot bear to cause him pain
day after day, only to be asked again
when I return.
Everyone says I must learn to lie.

Yes, Daddy. I beam a smile at him.
He had to work today.

Clock Face

I watched my grandmother's descent.
Standing barefoot by the road
with her purse slung over her arm,
waiting for no one,
lost in her own driveway.

Forgetting where her bathroom was
or how to turn off the stove burner.
Not recalling how much she loved coffee.
She spent her final days
in a nursing home, drinking
rotgut decaf from a beige cafeteria cup.

My mother feared the worst.
She saw her future in her mother's face:
  blank expression,
    confusion,
      anger,
        paranoia,
          submission to the inevitable.

Eight years later her own descent
began its sinister spiral. Took three tries
before we found the right doctor,
the one who asked the right question:
Can you draw a clock face?

She couldn't do it,
try as she might.
Her clock was worthy of Dali,
not round at all.
The hours jumbled together,
uneven, out of place, out of time.

And now, every morning,
as I drink my coffee
and savor every swallow,
I draw a clock face
on my paper napkin
for her and for me.

Magic

Miss Rita was not a beautician.
She was a sorceress, a magical being.
Grinding her mortar and pestle.
Mixing elixirs and pastes
　　to transform gray-haired ladies
　　into fresher versions of themselves
　　in less than two hours.
Restoring their youthful appearances
　　for at least a month.

Shearing away tangled knots
　　twisted during the night
　　by Queen Mab herself.
Conjuring poisonous potions that made eyes water,
　　one to drench curling rods with its foul stench,
　　one to neutralize with its sweeter scent.
All stored away in bottles and tubes
　　in a closeted room
　　filled with secret mixtures.
Instruments to brush, to cut, to transfigure
　　the coven of ladies who aired their grievances
　　and gossiped about their latest victims.
All that was missing was a spell.

A young apprentice appeared from nowhere
　　with her long, black broom.
She swept cast-off locks of hair
　　into a white and silver swirl
　　before adding wisps of red, brown, and blonde
while Miss Rita worked her enchantments.

The coven members brought in glossy magazines

with pictures of celebrities
they longed to emulate.
They sat for hours under blowing winds
of heated domes
like Circe's sisters,
hoping to change themselves
into someone else.

At last, with their hair colored and twisted in curls
and their eyebrows waxed,
the ladies peered into the mirror and wondered:
Who's the fairest of them all?
Each of them left the beauty shop
with a smile,
convinced she was the one.

The Garden Country Club

Square family plots
with low marble walls
appear like patchwork among clusters
of Black-eyed Susans
and blue asters along a country road.

Faded silk flowers in concrete vases
flank weathered headstones inscribed
with names and dates.
Carpets of gravel chips
cover the recumbent residents of
their newfound community.

People brought together
from all walks of life,
laid to rest with one another.
A man who died
when his tractor rolled over him.
A twenty-something killed
when a private plane crashed
on the way to a family reunion.

A physician who brought
hundreds of babies into the world.
Teen drivers who made one mistake.
Housewives, farmers, salesmen, teachers,
soldiers, lawmen, criminals, preachers.
Some who cherished their years,
and some who decided to end them.
Most with nothing in common but death.

Wealthy, poor, educated, uneducated.
Lives ended too soon by disease while
others lived to the fullness of their years.

Bitter disputes ended.
Family ties broken,
though buried side by side.
Whispers from visitors about the deceased:
We musn't speak ill of the dead.

Members of an exclusive group,
the one most didn't ask to join,
lie facing toward the East,
dressed in their finest,
awaiting the Day of Resurrection.

In different times and places,
their paths might never have crossed,
but now they hobnob
in their garden country club.

Caleb

He flew away a young man
and returned a troubled soul.
One who found solace
    at the bottom of a glass
    of mountain moonshine.
Not that he hadn't looked there before.

All his years he loved to fish,
whiling away hours in his boat,
drifting on the soft currents of wild lakes,
bobbing on the surface of a life
that threatened to drown him.
A human form defying surface tension
    and the laws of physics.

Peering deep into murky water,
    he searched for hungry bass
    and answers to a question:
What lay ahead for him in the future?

PTSD, like a savage animal, hiding,
    waiting for the perfect moment
    to pounce on its prey.
A heavy concrete abutment
    of a highway bridge on the way home
    from his visit to a veteran's hospital.
The twisted wreckage of his truck
    where his life came to an end.

A country boy who left home
    for the steamy jungles of Vietnam.
A soldier who hung beneath a helicopter,
    defying the laws of gravity.

A warrior suspended in mid-air, his hands
    holding a deadly rapid-fire weapon
    shooting at enemy targets
    in an aerial ballet of death.
A seeker who found the answer to his question
    a decade later,
    not in Vietnam,
    but on a two-lane highway
    in rural Georgia.

With a deep scar
    from a bullet wound to his foot,
invisible damage to his psyche,
    and a Purple Heart for his injury,
with acceleration and momentum
of tires screeching and metal striking
    solid concrete head-on,
    he proved the truth
    of Newton's third law of motion.

The troubled warrior,
    dressed as a civilian,
    lay in state
    in the local funeral home,
a patriot honored in death when honor
    was denied to the living.
Medals and ribbons of every color
clung to a thin, dried oak branch
that rested alongside his body.

Not one of the accolades lay pinned on his chest,
    as if showing his pride and respect,
    yet keeping his awards at a distance.
A reminder that he served his country,
but his country did not serve him.

The Preacher

Eleven o'clock.
Time to start acting
like a fiery evangelist.

Pounding his hands on
the pulpit like he was
driving out evil.
Beating his fist
on the Holy Bible
like he was cleansing
the sins of his congregation
the way a washerwoman
beats soapy bedsheets against a rock
to clear away the dirt.

Folks worked hard all week,
went to church on Sunday,
kept the Sabbath Day holy.

Families gathered for dinner.
Platters of fried chicken,
bowls of dried butterbeans
boiled with fatback,
deviled eggs, sliced ruby-red tomatoes,
cornbread with a little bacon grease
to help it brown up nice.

They held each other's hands
and said prayers of thanksgiving
to their loving God—
not the one The Preacher yelled about
in every sermon.

Fire and brimstone
with no room for love.

God wasn't angry,
but The Preacher was.

The Shot Lady

One by one,
hapless children formed a line,
their faces filled with dread,
their hearts filled with trepidation.
The group made its way
down the hallway to the library,
at other times, a pleasant place to be,
but not that day.

Syringes placed in perfect rows,
gleaming silver on a white tablecloth,
ready for inoculations.
Ampules of smallpox vaccine
lurked nearby, to be scratched
on each child's left arm
by a woman dressed in white,
the one they all called
The Shot Lady.
Her nurse's cap perched
at a precarious angle
on her salt-and-pepper hair.

Clinical, almost soulless,
with a mission to complete
for the county health department,
she must vaccinate them all.
Public school students
with no say in their destiny.

As the line inched toward the table,
their anxiety swelled to a crescendo
that throbbed with each heartbeat.

Watching the hysteria
of needle-phobic classmates,
an occasional child
fell ill or fainted on the spot.
A few never made it past
the cotton swabs of alcohol
on their arms.

No lollypops for good boys and girls.
No soothing words.
One single syllable: *Next!*

Their classroom teacher, never married,
most motherly of all,
whispered words of comfort
and hugged terrified children,
telling them to close their eyes.
They buried their fearful faces
against her blue, pearl-buttoned sweater.

Later, traveling home on the bus,
children chattered
about the horrors of their day.
They waited for the smallpox scratch
to turn into a festering sore
that would turn dark and ache all week
before leaving a lifelong scar.

Adults saw the day's work
as the good outweighing the bad,
and no one developed the deadly diseases.
But no one ever asked the frightened
children for their opinions.

No one thought to explain to them
the who and why before the fell swoop
of syringes and apprehension
descended on a sunny room
filled with the smell of classic books,
leaving behind the pervasive fumes
of alcohol mixed with tears.

The school children learned that day.
Instilled with fears of needles and nurses,
they learned to grow more wary
of seeing The Shot Lady's car
through a peaceful classroom window.

Aunt Eris

She was one of those relatives
who caused pure dread
when her car pulled up
on the rocky dirt driveway
at my grandmother's house.

Unannounced, of course,
just a man and his wife
with nothing to do on a Sunday
afternoon but drop in
on unsuspecting kinfolks for a visit.
She made stomachs twist into knots
wherever she visited.

Even her only daughter
had poor tolerance when it came
to her mother's constant criticism.
Eris could turn a bright summer day
into a dark, cloudy afternoon
when there weren't any clouds at all.

Gossiping. Complaining.
Bringing her own version
of her namesake, the goddess
of discord, to my widowed
grandmother's cheerful kitchen.

Mama asked Daddy,
Why is she still alive?
He took only two seconds
to pull the answer from his mind.
Well, I reckon it's
'cause the Devil
don't want her.

But the day came when the Devil
had no choice. Eris had to go somewhere.
After the funeral, Daddy shook his head.
I have no doubt she's complaining
about her new accommodations.

Virgil's Hand

He raised his hand to ask permission
and slinked out of the classroom
to the dirty toilet down the hall.

He raised his hand to answer a question.
The teacher looked the other way.
It wasn't the first time.

He raised his hand and shouted *Hallelujah!*
when he gave his heart to the Lord.
Everyone else was doing the same.

He raised his hand and promised loyalty
when he swore allegiance
to fight for the flag he loved.

He raised his hand to affirm an oath
for his new government job
with benefits and a pension.

He raised his hand to admire his glass,
hoping whiskey would bring
clarity to his clouded psyche.

He raised his hand to menace and strike
his children, full force
against their fearful faces.

He raised his hand to slap his wife,
to affirm his dominance
in a house filled with rage.

With the silver flash of a butcher knife
    clenched in the fist of a woman
    tired of his abuse,
    Virgil never raised his hand again.

Irises

Emerald blades rise like jagged swords
along the marble edge of an old family plot.
Perhaps irises flourished here years ago,
but what color will they be
if they decide to bloom again?

Barely surviving now, neglected,
they once graced this shady spot
where a dozen family members
lie forever in peace.
No one remembers who planted them
or when their flags first appeared.
There is no one to ask.
Perhaps the gardener rests among the others
in this garden of death.

The blades are flat and fan-like.
Some rhizomes are buried
far too deep to send up stems.
Others are lying half-buried on the ground,
their tubers never piercing
a hole in the dark soil,
yet resting easy while their roots
continue to work.

We dig up a few to take home.
No one will mind.
There is no one left to mind.
We will plant them in memory
of relatives who went before us.

But what color will their flowers be?
My sister guesses white.
Passing months will tell us—
if the roots choose to take hold
in the garden of the living.

Note to Myself

I can see the boy standing
there, looking down
on the graves
of his cousins,
his grandmother,
his grandfather—
the one who smoked unfiltered
Camels or rolled his own
with crimp-cut tobacco
from a can.

The boy pays his respects
at the grave of another man,
his father—
the one who couldn't quit
his two-packs-a-day habit
and begged the boy not to start.

Yet the boy and his cousin
hid behind the barn,
smoking rabbit tobacco
before moving on
to the real thing.

The boy looks just like me.
Hell, he *is* me.
My younger self.
What would I tell him
if I could warn him?

Cigarettes as standard issue
to GIs in Vietnam.
Two tours of duty
and thousands of smokes

doled out to soldiers like candy.
I was smoking my life away,

thinking I was fighting
the illusive enemy,
the Viet Cong.
The enemy was right there
all that time in my rations
and in my pocket.
I was cocky and invincible,
that kid standing there
now looking down
on a spot of bare earth.

He drops the butt of a half-smoked
cigarette on the ground
and grinds it into the dirt
with his cordovan penny loafer.
Eighteen years old
and new as that penny himself,
on his way to join the Army.

Hold onto that shiny penny, kid.
You're gonna need
all the luck you can get.
Stay away from cigarettes.
For the love of God,
stay away from looking cool.
Or one day you'll be
the dying man I am now.

Note to myself:
I never listened to my father.
I never listened to my wife.
I never listened to anyone.

Even if I could go back in time
and talk to the kid,
would the younger me
take my advice?

Must be the morphine.
I'm not dead yet,
but there's that plot of ground
lying like an enemy ambush,
waiting for a six-foot grave,
waiting for me—unless my wife
carries out her threat
to cremate my body
and scatter my ashes
in our barnyard
among the chicken scratch.
It would serve me right.

Oliver

Lord, he was handsome
sitting there in church clothes,
his shiny black hair gracing
his brow with a widow's peak.

Leaned back in a kitchen chair,
its white paint worn from use,
he sipped his coffee from a
chipped Blue Willow saucer.
Didn't bother him any—
her coffee tasted just as good.

He had already milked the cow
and put out fresh hay for the mule.
She had fed the chickens and gathered
brown eggs from the fussy biddies.
Farm work still had to go on,
even on a Sunday morning.

He worked all week in the cotton mill,
keeping a sharp eye on the bobbins,
hoping to save all his fingers
so he could play his guitar
on the porch on warm summer nights.

He could strum music that
made the angels jealous
before they gave in and sang along.
They seemed to prefer the blues,
and a Hank Williams song slipped
in every now and then.

Sometimes he danced with his gal in the yard

to the sound of music no one else could hear.
The yellow porch light shone behind them,
and they dissolved into waltzing silhouettes.

Beams of golden moonlight streamed from
the night sky, creating shadows of two lovers
on bare dirt swept clean with a brush broom.
Embracing away the world's pain,
a husband and wife with five young children,
trying to find joy in hard times.

Calligraphy

Miss Alma loved the magic
of hand-written words.
The fancy, the flourish,
ascenders and descenders,
majuscule and minuscule.

She taught us a hand
of cursive font.
She said we're judged
by the way we write,
and sending notes to others
in our best handwriting
is more than mere flair.
It is a gift of art,
a sign of respect.

Q and D or W and Z,
loops of b and p,
triple and double
humps of m and n.
The purposeful crossing
of x or dotting each
i and j with precision.

We scribed with fine nibs
of leaky fountain pens,
our fingers smudged with black,
our ink and ideas
blending on milk-white paper
in wispy swirls and twists.
Letters slanted to the right
in perfect italic style,
sensing their master's pen

might someday wield
power over tyrants.

Elegant strands of letters,
serif and sans-serif,
etched into fibers
of parchment or linen.
Now seen as cryptic shapes,
like hieroglyphics
scratched on rolls of papyrus,

indecipherable to many
who were never taught
or who never tried to learn,
those who cast aside
graceful elegance
for their own devices—
dull plastic keyboards
and wiggling emojis.

Miss Blanche

She never married
or had children of her own.
But year after year, she influenced
the lives of students
who found themselves
in her third grade classroom.

She spoke with a soft voice,
yet raised it to a firmer pitch if need be.
Always positive, never degrading.
Fresh flowers in a vase on her desk.
Perhaps, she believed, they were
the only beauty her students would see.

A mother figure, bandages and a box of tissues
at the ready. Extra pencils and paper.
No admonishments. Her students
were rural. School supplies
sat far down on parents' lists.

She taught in the same classroom
year after year. Forty years, to be exact.
Her students never used her last name.
In fact, they didn't know it.
She was always Miss Blanche,
to her students and adults alike,
a sign of respect and admiration.

And when she died at eighty-seven,
church friends and a few remaining relatives
graced the funeral service with their presence,
yet the pews were somehow full.

In his eulogy, the pastor asked the congregation,
How many of you were taught by Miss Blanche?
Most everyone stood, students from years past.
It seems Miss Blanche had children after all.

Vergie

Afraid of her own shadow, she was.
Buzzing wasps sent her into a frenzy.
Change of any kind was anathema.
Simple spices burned her tongue.
Their fragrant scents disgusted her,
and anyone who sprinkled pepper
became an object of her scorn.

Her children were an annoyance.
Her grandchildren unnerved her.
Dogs and cats were not welcome—
she hoped they would all disappear.
A visit to anywhere left her in a state
of panic and dyspepsia.

Covered bridges reeked of danger,
and strangers of any ethnicity
set her on a trail of mistrust and fright.
Stack upon stack of dishes to be washed
after three full meals a day
led to an endless array
of obsessions in her kitchen.

She scrubbed the dishes with fierceness
to eliminate all grease and germs.
The sight of water spots on knives
pushed her anxiety over the edge.
Worry and malaise dogged her nights.
Her husband dogged her days.

She imposed her phobias and dictates
on her offspring with impunity.
They struggled for years to overcome

the emotional damage she instilled in them,
to find their own ways in the world.

A fear-filled life, yet with no regrets
for whiling away all her days
in a haze of misery and unfounded dread.
And in the end, after ninety-five years,
Death took her on an adventure
she did not wish to take.

Fred's Molasses

The mule proved to be adequate,
worthy of the farmer's cash.
He wore his blinders and plodded
ahead, obeying repeated calls
of *gee* and *haw*, his heavy plow
digging deep, unsteady furrows
ready for planting sorghum seeds
in a fallow field of red dirt.

In time, promising stalks
sprouted from fertile soil.
Hope and anticipation sprang up
with the emerging growth.

Maybe amber drizzles to sweeten
hot biscuits, right out of the oven,
slathered with churned, creamy butter
melting across their crusts.

Maybe confections devoured
by laughing children pulling taffy,
casting aside all concerns for their teeth.

Maybe a spoonful of whiskey dotted
with the sugary, sticky liquid to calm
a vexing cough on a winter's night.

Persevering through the summer heat and storms,
the plants grew higher until the time was right
to slash away their leaves and harvest their canes.
All Fred needed to do was follow a lead rope
and walk in circles around the sorghum mill,
pulling a log behind him as a counterbalance.

The log would turn creaking rollers,
crushing pile after pile of thick stalks,
pressing out green liquid destined to be boiled
over a fire until it became molten heaven.

Fred had other ideas; he saw nothing desirable
in the back-breaking work and sweaty faces
of humans laboring in the heat, slapping away flies,
straining, stirring, and swirling wooden paddles.
The humans were no different from him.

He saw no reason to work himself to death.
He imagined his destiny lay elsewhere,
and after only one day of going round and round,
he decided for himself he'd had enough
of clomping in never-ending, pointless circles.

With a hard, calamitous kick
and resounding brays that pierced the quiet
of a sunny September afternoon,
he tore away one side of his make-shift corral
near the smoke and heavy sweetness.

Freed at last, he headed at full gallop
toward the lush grass of the pasture
and took a long drink of water
from the edge of an inviting lake.

He watched a pair of mallards
paddling in the ripples his thirst created.
He longed to be free like the ducks
and feel the warmth of the sunrise
every morning in the open field.

The frustrated farmer shook his head
and led the mule inside the barn.
Fred remained still long enough
to pose for the farmer's camera.

A label with the mule's picture
graced every jar of molasses
the farmer sold: *Fred's Molasses*.
Fred might have been a mule all right,
but he didn't want to be one.

The Suitcase

Elizabeth entered the world
on Christmas Day in 1926.
Twenty-one months later,
in the midst of a September drought,
she sat in her highchair at breakfast
as her brother hurried off to school.

By two o'clock, family members
brought him home to sorrow.
His sister had left the world
on that late-summer afternoon.

Diphtheria, relentless and lethal,
stole her from her mother's arms.
Within hours a train from Atlanta
pulled in at the depot in Bullochville
bringing doses of vaccine,
too late for Elizabeth,
but just in time for her brother.

For weeks, the late summer rains
had not fallen on the parched cotton field
that stretched out beside the homeplace.

Imprints of little bare feet
lingered for days afterward
in the soft, red dirt
before the rains fell
and washed away the memories.

Time passed, and sixty years later
her mother slipped away to glory.
The day came to clear the house,
to climb a ladder to the loft.

A nephew Elizabeth never knew
lowered items to the floor:
Two faded wooden chairs, a clock covered
with columns of dried dirt dauber nests,
rusty black kerosene lanterns,
and a battered brown suitcase
lying silent under decades of dust,
about to give up its secrets.

Everyone knew about the suitcase,
but no one had ever opened it
to see what lay inside.

Not silver or gold,
not diamonds or rubies,
but treasures from a little girl
who never lived to see
her second birthday.

Painted metal dishes from
a child's tea set.
Empty face powder boxes
that were special because
they belonged to Mama.
A small, much-loved cloth doll.

Sacred treasures kept safe,
all painful reminders
of journeys never taken,
gleeful laughter silenced,
a life never lived and frozen in time.

A toddler's playthings
tucked away in a suitcase
by her grieving mother.
A tiny angel's memories
tucked away in her mother's heart.

Lizzie

She's gone now.
Two bossy relatives
went through drawers and closets,
filled bags with giveaways,
stuffed another one with discards
to haul to the trash.

Wait.

I cannot believe
they were going to throw this away.
Tattered places in the cotton fabric,
frayed edges here and there.
Her DNA embedded in the strings
she tied day after day
with arthritic fingers now lying still.

Stains.

Tea, blackberry cobbler, country ham,
red-eye gravy, Japanese fruit cake.
When she wore that apron,
she was cooking something special.

Respect.

She's gone to glory.
Time to save her apron.
Rescue it from the shame
of a black garbage bag.

Treasure.

My grandmother's apron
is coming home with me.

John

Low-hanging leafy branches
cast heavy blue-gray shadows
on a clear stream,
its source bubbling near the edge
of the homeplace property line.

A fine spot to run off moonshine.
Bags of sugar, mighty hard to get
during the War, lay nearby.
He had his secret sources.

He never sold his whiskey. He wasn't
a bootlegger at heart, so he
chose to drink it all himself,
except with a few special friends—

the ones who knew he made
good shine, not rotgut
they would come to regret.

Friends who could be trusted not
to turn him over to the revenuers.
Sometimes his plow sat still
in the field, the old mule's brain
left befuddled in his blinders,

wondering why his owner had
stopped plowing the rows of furrows
and left him standing there alone
to take a long break from his work.

Sitting under a sweet gum tree,
pulling deep swigs from a pint
jar that once held peaches, John
swallowed his prize whiskey
to wash away dust and regrets.

Conversations with a Storyteller

How many stories you reckon you've told?

Quite a few, I reckon, the storyteller replied.

The storyteller is gone, but I'm still here.
I talk to him every now and again when I'm alone.
I want him to know I remember him
and I'm keeping his stories.

Roll that Prince Albert cigarette
with your yellow-stained fingers.
Sit with me in the porch swing,
look off toward the mountains.

Tell me about the day you went away to war,
a young man full of fire and vinegar.
You were gonna save the world
in the war to end all wars.
You hoped to travel overseas
and see a bit of the world you saved
with your buddies, clutching
whiskey bottles and glory.

Life took a sharp turn in training.
Rumbling guns shook your eardrums.
You never left stateside.
Back home at twenty-two.
Back home to plow cotton fields
and bubble up some moonshine.
Wear that wired-up hearing aid
for the rest of your life.
Settle into marriage. Settle.

Sit with me in the present
and take me back to your past.
Tell me about the times you walked with ease
along the banks of a fern-lined branch
hunting for turtles with your hooked stick
or robbing wild black honeybee hives.

Tell me about the days you could walk
without your cedar cane and a slow shuffle,
before the strokes set in
and robbed you of your vigor.

In hard cold winters, feed heart pine lighter
into the pot-bellied stove to warm yourself.
Toss in a few unshelled pecans to roast
in the edges of red and ash-gray embers.

How many stories you reckon you've forgot?

Never could read much.
Never wrote 'em down.

That's a shame, ain't it?
I would've liked to hear 'em.
Tell me one you remember, Grandpa.

Wispy white hair
and a gravelly, halting voice.
I always thought you were old.
You lay down for the last time at sixty-eight,
same age as me now.

Reckon how many stories you took with you?
That's a shame, ain't it?

Wild Black Honeybees

The child had no idea her grandfather stuttered.
It was years later when an older gentleman
making polite conversation
at a relative's funeral visitation told the adult,
I knew your grandfather years ago.
He related a story her grandfather once told him
about an encounter with wild black honeybees.

He was in the woods robbing their hive for honey.
He used his honeybee smoker to calm them down.
but it didn't work as he had planned.
The bees came after him with a vengeance.
He had to run away as fast as he could
to jump in a nearby mountain creek.

The gentleman asked him, *I bet that hurt, didn't it?*
Her grandfather replied,
It s-s-s-sure d-d-did!.

The man meant no harm.
He was true to what he heard.
The granddaughter was puzzled.
Her aunt confirmed the answer.
Yes, baby, your grandfather did stutter.

But the child had never noticed.
She was far more interested
in what her grandfather had to say,
passing his stories down to her
in the front porch swing.
Stories that had no concern
for his stuttering words
that transcended pauses and uneasiness
and lived on after he was gone.

Perhaps he was comfortable sitting
with his young granddaughter
in his swing on quiet afternoons,
free to share his history without judgment
or the harshness of expectations.

The New Straw Hat

Two brothers sat together
on the rough wood seat
watching their old mule
pull their rickety wagon.
Its wheels stirred up dust
as it rolled down the road
on a dry summer afternoon.
They had been to the feed store
over in The Valley to buy supplies,
plus a brand new straw hat
George bought with his own money.

Their parents were hard at work
down the way on the family farm.
Their mother hummed
as she went about her work,
hanging wet clothes on the line
while their father hoed weeds
in the cotton field. The boys
needed to get on back home
and help their father.

Their mule, Gray Baby,
was a friend of the family.
How many hours had the boys
spent, walking in their brogans
behind the mule and plow?
At night in fitful sleep,
they called out, *Gee! Haw!*

George was sporting his new straw hat.
In fact, he thought it was a fine hat,
especially for only twenty-five cents.

His older brother Grady
was holding the reins,
mischief dancing in his eyes.

For Gray Baby, like any mule,
any time was the right time
to raise her tail
and do her business.

Sure enough, just as she lifted her tail,
Grady snatched his brother's hat
and held it under the mule's tail.

Sudden shouts of anger
pierced the quiet air
and interrupted their mother's song.
Looking up the road,
she saw her sons
rolling in the dirt,
fists flying,
a straw hat cast aside.
What in the world?

The mule ambled
on down the hill,
pulling the empty wagon,
leaving the boys
to continue their yelling.

Not understanding the fuss,
Gray Baby didn't seem to care
what was happening,
but she wanted no part of it.

She knew the direction
she was going,
and she knew the way home,
even if the humans
seemed to have lost their way.

She didn't understand fighting.
All she wanted was water,
shade, and a peaceful place to rest.

Ella's Quilt

A young Methodist pastor
answered God's call
to the other side of the country.
I asked if he needed a bedspread
for Pacific Northwestern nights.

No, I would rather have
your great-grandmother's quilt.

After three generations in our family,
Ella's quilt had journeyed down to me.
It hung on a wooden quilt rack,
honored in its special place
for twenty-five years.
Time to pass it down.

Ella was a beginning-to-end woman.
A wildcrafter of leaves and roots
for herbal medicines and teas.
A rural midwife who birthed
seven children of her own.

She formed a sisterhood of women
who called on her to help them
bring new lives into the world.
In times of death, neighbors sent for her
to dress women's bodies for burial.

I never knew her.
I wish I had.

Her quilt made no claims
to be an artistic piece of work,

but it came to life with her hands.
She cut the squares and triangles,
laid out her pattern,
and fashioned unique patchworks
she sewed together one by one.

Material from her daily life—
leftover scraps from dresses
she made or cloth from feed sacks
she saved for future quilts.

She finished her quilt
by hand-stitching these words
and the year in a corner square:
Mother Smith 1933.

She didn't stitch *Ella.*
Her quilt was more than a project
to while away wintry hours.
It was her gift for the future.
She wanted to be remembered
as a mother, a matriarch.
She died the next year.
The old quilt winged its way
from our local post office
to the Evergreen State.
It traveled farther in one day
than Ella traveled in her lifetime.

On long winter nights,
my son now sleeps
under the warmth of Ella's quilt,
covered by love
passed down to him
from a woman who,

more than eighty years before,
stitched her chosen name
and passed along a creation
of enormous work—
the fabric of our family.

A benediction
from Mother Smith
for a great-great-grandson
she would never know.

In Memoriam

One by one
they drop from the sky
and find their perches among
thin, lithe boughs
of a leafless white oak tree,
now a sharp silhouette sketched in inky black lines
against an ominous steel-gray sky.

Only a few stubborn patches of lichen
dare to cling here or there like crepe
left behind on the empty branches.
Dried sunflowers in the garden
hang their heads in grief and disbelief.
They know their end has come.

The mourners are wearing their funereal finest.
Sleek, ebony feathers reflect the slanted rays of
the afternoon sun but find no warmth in this place.
Shiny, black eyes survey the sight below them.
One of their own, felled by the farmer's gun,
is strung from a rope on the barbwire fence.
A warning, a sign to his kindred.
They are not welcome here.
They might share his fate.

In solemn respect the mourners sit in silence,
a brief corvine ceremony of peace and respect.
Then all at once the service concludes
as if some unseen chorus master has waved his baton.
They lift their wings and fly away together,
each one calling out to one another
in discordant voices only they understand.
A benediction for their fallen comrade.

Japanese Iris

I wish you could have seen it,
blooming by the lake—
a Japanese iris you planted,
rising first among the others,
still a day too late.

You waited.
You hoped.
You expected
deep lavender petals,
unfurling flags
lifting their standards
to the golden morning sun.

You never saw the iris
nodding in the breeze
at the edge of the water,
raising emerald foliage upward
like thin benevolent swords
proclaiming victory over the
darkness of the soil that birthed it.

An afternoon shower began to fall.
Raindrops slipped down
into the beardless bloom.
The iris lowered its head
and wept with us.
I wish you could have seen it.

Shadow Dance

Sunlight peers
through wispy clouds high
above a blanket of flowers.
Butterflies flutter about
to taste the sunflowers,
to catch a glimpse of beauty
captured by sorrow's reach.

Not far away
a rooster crows
and breaks the solemnity
with his call for a new day.

She would have loved
the glorious passion
of nature's condolences.
The butterflies' wings.
The blue sky scattered
with clouds scudding by
in a hurry, creating
the sun's shadow dance.

The guest singer crows again
from atop a barnyard fence,
his beak open like a trumpet,
crowing his morning song,
crowing his mourning song.
It's eleven o'clock on a Thursday,
and they've all come to say good-bye.

Minerva and Dixie

They never owned a car.
That didn't matter—
they never learned to drive.
Lack of transportation
posed no problem at all.

They walked to work every day,
just down the way, to be shuttered inside
for grueling shifts at the cotton mill.

Their small white house stood
in Mill Village along a shady street
where country nieces and nephews liked
to visit and bring their roller-skates
to glide unimpeded on the pavement
and jump the cracks in the sidewalk.

Dixie, timid and soft-spoken,
lived her life in peace and simplicity.
Her red hair ablaze, she expressed grace
through inquiring green eyes
framed with gold wire-rims and innocence.

Minerva, her opinionated older sister,
showed a quick wit and a ready retort,
a feisty spirit with no patience
toward those she deemed dull.
Her young forever love, her fiancé,
snatched away from her years before
while in service to his country.

A one-pound coffee can sat tucked away
in a dark corner of every room,

discreet places to spit liquid brown snuff.
Embroidered handkerchiefs, hidden in pockets,
touched their lips and kept them spotless.
Dipping snuff, but proper women, nonetheless.

On quiet evenings, in front of the fireplace
in the chilly house, shiny black dominoes lay
spread out on a card table, aligned
in rows and junctions, connecting the dots,
yet never quite so with their lives.

Two sisters, never married.
After fifty years of labor among spools,
thread, fabric, and whirring machinery,
each earned herself a watch with diamonds,
timepieces to tick away their remaining time.

Dixie spent her final weeks
slipping in and out of foggy mists
ushered in by lingering nights in a nursing home.
After a life lived in frugality and humble faith,
she made no extravagant requests.
All she wanted was a baby doll to hold.

Minerva wouldn't allow it.
It would be silly
and embarrassing
for an old woman
to do such a thing.

After all, they were ladies.
What would people think?

Memory in a Bottle

One small bag
was all Mama brought
    to spend the night at my house.

I peered into her room.
She sat in silence on the foot
    of the bed
and remained there
    for more than an hour
    in her khaki pants and
    flowery pullover shirt.

Each time I checked on her,
she was sorting through items
    in her bag
    over and over,
pondering each one of them
    as if to make sense of them all.

A comb, a brush, her precious lipstick.
(Every Southern lady must own a lipstick.)
Undergarments, a soft pink cotton nightgown,
    and a sweater.

She was always cold, no matter what the season.
I convinced her to change clothes
    and put on my warmest robe.
She seemed to linger forever in the bathroom.
Half an hour to change
    into a simple gown and robe.
Half a decade to change into someone
    I no longer knew.

At last she opened the door
    and appeared in the hallway
    dressed for bed.
A soft perfume surrounded her.

Lavender and jojoba oil,
my lotion on the bathroom counter.
She'd rubbed some of the quieting elixir
    on her hands and face.
I hope it brought her comfort
    and gave her peaceful sleep.

A dozen years later I still keep
    the half-empty bottle
    on my writing desk.

Sometimes I open it
to release its luxurious scent,
    and for a moment
    its fragrance brings
    her back to me.

Mama

She was always dressed to the nines,
colors coordinated, with shoes to match,
adorned with earrings and a string of pearls,
a brooch pinned on her jacket.
She had her hair teased and styled
every Thursday afternoon
in her favorite beauty salon,
its air thick with hairspray and gossip.

A business woman who processed checks
and headed the payroll department,
she worked her magic with arithmetic
on an electric calculator
long before desktop computers arrived.

Now she wore a sweater—someone else's sweater—
and khaki pants. Thick white socks she won at Bingo
and laced-up orthopedic shoes. Nothing matched.
She confused members of her family.
She argued when furniture in the parlor was moved
because she thought it belonged to her.
Her brother drove from states away to visit.
The next day she didn't remember he was there.
Staff members were kind to her.

Hanging on the wall outside her doorway
an empty eight-by-ten photo frame
beckoned to be filled.
The facility director suggested helpfully,
Perhaps you can bring a recent picture
of your mother. One from happier times.

Her daughter chose a different photograph,
her parents in 1943. Smiling, sitting together
in a grassy field, holding hands. A life full of promise
ahead of them—love, marriage, children, dreams.

A reminder to everyone there.
Once she was young and beautiful,
with a smile that lit up a room.
Not with a lost look,
her eyes filled with confusion.
Mismatched everything.

Once she was young.
Her life had purpose.
She mattered.
She still mattered.

A Good Woman

Her headstone stood
as a truth, a reminder
that she once existed.
She lived her span of years
before being laid to rest
in her church cemetery,
facing toward the East.

Her grave was graced
with the usual words
carved in granite.
Her name, her date of birth,
the date of her passing.
And below the dates,
the word *Mother*.

After many years,
her headstone had become
motley, streaked gray and drab green
from the passage of time
and weeping sap
from the old cedar tree
holding on to life nearby.

But the headstone did not
speak enough words. Its sparse
carving was elegant but empty.
Someone who loved her
built a low wooden form
around the gravestone's base
and poured cement there.
A finger inscribed three words
in the wet cement:
A Good Woman.

A costly headstone
chiseled in granite for a price.
A rough concrete addition
with an inscription from the heart.
Which was the greater testament
to a life well lived?

Lunch with the Family

One by one through the years
the Smiths have found their way here.
Now they rest together beneath orderly rows
of headstones in this country church cemetery,
        eighteen members in number,
        three generations before me,
        facing toward the East.

Some of them I knew while others I did not.
Their time began long before mine.
I know them only through family stories
and yellowed photographs.

Standing in reverence among their graves,
        I wonder about their lives.
I have questions I wish I could ask them
        and answers I will never know.

How many gallons of moonshine
        their stills ran off
        by a rippling fern-lined mountain stream
        flowing beneath low-growing branches and
        hidden away from the revenuer's sharp eyes.
How many hammers and nails,
        mules and plows,
        and garden seeds
        they used to make a living.
How many quilts the women stitched together,
        their nimble fingers pulling needles and thread
        through carefully measured pieces of fabric
        to keep their families warm on winters' nights
        when cold winds howled outside their doors.

How many fire and brimstone sermons they heard
before cheerfully returning home to sit around tables
with mismatched plates and glasses of sweet tea
set on farm tables covered with worn cotton tablecloths.
How many blessings they said to their loving God
(not the one they heard about in church)
to offer thanksgiving and to enjoy the fruits of their labor.
How many heaps of potato salad,
deviled eggs, and sliced juicy tomatoes
they ate for Sunday dinner.
How many pieces of chicken they fried,
chickens that were running about
in the yard the day before.
How many pans of banana pudding
under mountains of meringue,
or buttermilk cornbread johnny cakes
in black skillets seasoned with age,
cooked up nice in wood stoves.
How many pangs of childbirth they felt,
some ending with joy and some with weeping,
children lost at birth or felled by disease
in the short course of helpless days.
How many veterans proudly wore their uniforms
in service to our country
in Europe and Vietnam
and brought back scars
like broken souvenirs
lying on a shelf,
at last covered in dust.

My sister is visiting the family with me.
We decide it's time for lunch in my car.
We open paper bags and bring out
potato chips and ham sandwiches,
cold bottles of water, and paper napkins.

After our lunch with the family is finished,
we gather our bags and wrappings
and all the memories of loved ones passed
as if we carry them away with us in zip-locked bags,
as if to keep them fresh or so they cannot vanish.

I crank my car and we head on into town
to spend the afternoon with our aunt
who is pale and weak from strokes.
She will soon fly away
for a reunion of her own.
We want to visit with her one last time
before she joins the family for lunch.

The Visitor

Andrew died on an August afternoon.
Not by his own choosing,
but pulled away young by disease.
His death left her wondering
how she would go on,
how she could deal with such loss.

The house felt bereft.
No laughter, no music, only grief.
Lowered voices, the breath
of her sleeping dog,
and the relentless tick, tick of a clock
marked the passing of each day.

Until that first night
when the visitor paid a call.
Black swirling smoke,
a presence rolling
low to the floor
down the empty hallway.

No shadow, no noise.
Just the thin mist of an entity.
Her daughter saw him
from time to time.
He never caused them harm.
He became a frequent guest,
so they gave him a name—Ned.

His visits continued
until one night,
when shapeless wisps
crept along the floor,

she placed both hands on her hips
and told the visitor
it was time for him to go.
Time for her
to get back to living.
And Ned never came back.

Vesta

If I tell you this is true,
you'll laugh and call me a liar.
Truth is an unwelcome stranger
in a world where people love lies.

Vesta was a ghost-seer, a dreamer,
burning sage to keep away the haints.
She'd tell them to move on down the road
or cross over to the light.
Though they came to her for help,
they weren't allowed to linger at her house.

She painted her front porch ceiling
the color of robin eggs in spring.
Sometimes, sitting in the porch swing,
she'd speak to wandering souls
and listen to their stories
whispered on a thin summer breeze.

Look up there. Can't you just see heaven?
Go toward the light. Your soul is finished
with all its troubles down here.
It's time for you to find your way.

It may seem cruel to send troubled spirits
on their way, but it's not right
to mislead them with false hope,
to let them wander the earth lost,
like wailing banshees, suffering
the sorrows of a second death.

Only Vesta's family knew
about her fearsome gift,
but now she's crossed over,
talking about her doesn't matter so much.

All I know is what I heard her say
when her kitchen turned cold
and damp on a hot summer afternoon,
when the wind was calm, the sun ablaze.

All I know is what I saw:
Her eyes, clear blue-green
like the water of a mountain lake,
staring beyond me to the otherworld.
Go on now, honey. You're done here.

If I tell you this is true,
you'll laugh and call me *touched.*
Maybe you'll study me with eyes
full of pity or disdain. You'll shake
your head and mumble to yourself,
Ain't no such.

Truth is an unwelcome stranger
in a world where people love lies.
Vesta was my grandmother,
and she passed her gift on down.

Uncle Billy

Vesta had a dream one night.
Her brother fell down, but he got up again.
He fell down once more, but he didn't get up.

Far away in Italy, far away from home
for a country farm boy, one of twelve children,
he was carrying weapons and fighting strangers,
many no older than he was.

Fascism had raised its ugly head.
Only twenty-three, a young wife back home,
and the weight of the war riding heavy
on his shoulders, enemy fire
shattered his youthful innocence.
Injured, but at least not dead.

Medics got him stable. He was recovering
in a hospital bed. A bomb dropped without
warning. Billy never got up.

One chilly February afternoon, the county vet
knocked on Vesta's front door.
Usually he came calling to care
for everybody's cows or dogs and cats.
That day he was visiting on official business.

Do you have a brother named Billy?
Puzzled, Vesta replied, *Yes, I do.*
With words cold and void of feeling,
he looked square at her and blurted out,
Not anymore. He got killed in the war.

Uncle Billy's parents received a telegram.
Their son was killed in a hospital bombing.
A few days later, they received
an earlier written telegram informing them
that their son was recovering in a hospital.
Grief compounded by wartime confusion.

An American flag, folded with dignity,
held a place of honor on their mantel.
Their son's flag. A son who died with honor.
Honor for one of many sons who gave their
full measure for the United States of America.
Sons who fell down but didn't get up.

Huckleberry Knob

We follow the trail uphill
and walk past thick foliage.
Our friend warns our group not
to touch the stinging nettles
that grow within hand's reach.
Wary eyes watch for snakes.
Our friend is a mountain woman,
and she knows Appalachian flora.
The nettles will cause itching and misery.

The hike takes us higher and higher.
At last we reach a grassy clearing, a bald,
but it is not our final stopping place.
We rest a few moments,
adjust our light backpacks,
and continue on the pathway
until we reach Huckleberry Knob.

Oddly, in this unexpected meadow,
we pass by a grave, a monument
to two young men who died in 1899
trying to hike across the mountain range
in severe winter weather, a poor decision
that ended their lives. Their bodies
and whiskey were discovered the next year.

The knob's panoramic view
of mountain ranges in the distance
inspires a new perspective:
Our existence becomes flat and empty
until we learn that our world
has more depth and breadth
to offer than we realize.

We live out our years as earth wanderers,
climbing upward, heading
for our final destination.
Sometimes we make questionable decisions.
We try to avoid the stings and misery.
We focus too much
on the unknowable future.
Too distracted by what is to come,
we hurry and forget the joy of the journey.

But here in the wide-open bald,
we sit on the grass
to rest and have lunch together,
friends sharing food and conversation.

Before we head back down
to our cars and the noise
of our everyday lives,
we ease into these moments
of renewal and peace.
We celebrate the *now*.

Warp and Weft

Up and down,
side to side,
I weave the threads
of my life like the
latitude and longitude
of my comings and goings.

I start from the beginning
with the line of prime meridian.
I weave the threads tight.
There must be no unraveling,
no knots, no open spaces
to let in the cold night air
of shallow days, of keen regrets.

Over time a design emerges
unique to me alone.
As I interlace the strands
in different shades of color,
some vibrant and some dark,
I wonder about my future
in the strands yet to be created.

When I am gone,
what will be left of me?
What will I leave behind
for my family?

I hope they will cherish
far more than earthly treasures
stored away in dusty drawers
or forgotten in old jewelry boxes.

I hope they will wrap themselves
in the warmth of who I was to them,
woven in the pattern of my fabric—
myself, in warp and weft.

Raven

Oh, how she loved honeybees.
Oh, how I love crows and frogs.
I gave her small gifts
to keep her spirits up.
Paper plates and napkins
imprinted with honeybees.
A bee key chain, a fairy light jar.
No matter how small the offerings,
she made a big deal about them.

She sent me greeting cards
with crows on the front.
I have no idea where she bought them.
I always used a honeybee emoji
by her name when I emailed her.
I signed with a green frog by my name.

We wrote back and forth,
a bee and a frog. She spelled
the word *be* in her emails b-e-e.
Every time.

Now, no more uplifting, fun emails.
No more telling me she wrote
to me in her heart, but she hadn't
written the words down yet.
Her bees have gone silent.
I knew she was ill. Six months to live,
but she added four more.

My son sent me an early Christmas
gift. He told me to call him when
the package arrived.

It appeared one afternoon in my mailbox.
A shiny blue envelope. I called him.
Open it, he said.

Inside was a golden honeybee necklace
and a card from the Honeybee Project.

I know what a hard time you've had
since her death. Read the card.
Go to that website, and you can name
a queen bee after her.

Through tears, I typed in the website address.
Now, somewhere near the Santa Monica Pier,
there's a hive with a queen bee named Raven.

When a Poet Dies

Unwritten poems float in mid-air.
Light as soft feathers, they swirl
in flights of fancy, disoriented
lost spirits lingering in expectation
before realizing their muse is gone.

They descend in sorrowful whispers
drifting down upon stricken souls
mourning one who embraced
life with extravagant passion—

unstifled by small-mindedness,
who looked into inscrutable darkness
and, with enlightened eyes and a visionary soul,
translated the lovely language of the universe.

The poet, in unfettered verse, foresaw the future
and engraved immortality on crackling pages
like mysterious treasure maps, their secret clues
pointing the way for us to follow.

When a poet dies, silhouettes penned in black ink
reach out from every orphaned word to remind us
of our endless pursuit of eternal truth,
even on the darkest of nights.

There is more to our destiny
than staring into empty cups
and brooding about our fate.

So we light the wick
and put our pen to paper
once again.

Acknowledgements

"Irises" previously appeared as a Poem of Merit in the 2020 edition of *The Reach of Song*, the annual poetry anthology published by the Georgia Poetry Society.

"Memory in a Bottle" appeared in the Journal of *chinaberrysummer.com*.

"Calligraphy" and "Warp and Weft" appeared in the online arts gallery of Delta Kappa Gamma Society International at dkg.org.

A children's version of "Ella's Quilt" was published in *Ella's Quilt*, a picture book published by Catch the Spirit of Appalachia, Inc. (2023). The quilt was passed down to the poet's son Zach in 2013 and is now ninety years old.

"In Memoriam" took second place in the Mnemosyne Award category of the 2018 Georgia Poetry Society fall contest. It appeared in *The Reach of Song*, the annual poetry anthology published by the Georgia Poetry Society.

Huckleberry Knob Trail is located near Robbinsville, North Carolina. Information about the history of the knob is posted on public signs near the entrance to the trail.

"Raven" honors the memory of the poet's friend and playwriting collaborator Raven Chiong who passed away in 2023.

"When a Poet Dies" honors the memory of poet Donald Newton "Newt" Smith, Jr., a writer, poet, and fellow member of North Carolina Writers' Network-West, who passed away in 2018.

Photos:
Thomas Andrew Barnett (1901-1954), photographer unknown
Grover Cleveland Smith (1892-1960), photographer unknown

Special thanks to Glenda Council Beall, Mary Ricketson, Carol Crawford, Pastor Zach Taylor, Lynn Burks Harbour, Susan Warner, and the North Carolina Writers' Network. With gratitude to members of my family who passed down stories and trusted me to be the keeper of our history. And much love to my husband Hugh who patiently lives with a wife who is always writing poetry in her head.

About the Author

Carroll S. Taylor grew up on a dirt road in rural Georgia. A graduate of Tift College, she is a writer, poet, and playwright. She is the author of two young adult novels, *Chinaberry Summer* and *Chinaberry Summer: On the Other Side* as well as two children's books, *Feannag the Crow* and *Ella's Quilt*. Her poems and stories have appeared in anthologies and online. Her plays have been performed onstage at the Peacock Performing Arts Center in Hayesville, North Carolina.

A retired educator, Taylor is a member of North Carolina Writers' Network and the Georgia Poetry Society. Snakes, turtles, lizards, and frogs often find their way into her writing. She and her husband Hugh live in Hiawassee, Georgia, where she feeds a visiting crow family whose antics inspire her to write every day.

Made in the USA
Middletown, DE
20 August 2024

59461837R00066